The Journey Back to Life

How I Took It One Day at a Time to Recover

Mark Elliott Toussaint

Copyright © 2026 Mark Elliott Toussaint

All rights reserved.

No part of this book may be reproduced, distributed, stored in a retrieval system, or transmitted in any form or by any means, electronic, mechanical, photocopying, recording, or otherwise, without the prior written permission of the author, except in the case of brief quotations used in reviews or scholarly works.

This book is a work of nonfiction based on the author's personal experiences. Names, locations, and identifying details have been changed in some cases to protect the privacy of individuals.

The views and opinions expressed in this book are those of the author and do not necessarily reflect the views of any organization, church, or recovery group. This book is not intended as a substitute for professional medical, psychological, or legal advice. Readers should consult qualified professionals regarding any medical, mental health, or recovery-related concerns.

ISBN: 978-1-968098-33-9

First Edition

Printed in the United States of America

Chapters

Introduction 1
1 A Life Before the Drugs 4
2 The First High 7
3 When Control Was Lost 11
4 The Jail Cell 14
5 Blind to Grace 17
6 Relapse 19
7 Detox, Institutions, and Despair 22
8 The Disease That Waits 25
9 Losing Everything 27
10 My Grandmother 29
11 The Breaking Point 31
12 Surrender 33
13 AA, NA, and the Steps 35
14 Mental Health 37
15 A New Mind 39
16 Fourteen Years Sober 41
17 Ministry 43
18 Family Restored 45
19 What God Taught Me 47
20 For the One Still Using 49
Epilogue: One Day at a Time 51

Introduction

My name is Mark Elliott Toussaint, and this is the story of how I came out of a hopeless state by taking simple suggestions in a program that required only one thing from me: honesty with myself.

Addiction does not discriminate. It does not care where you come from, how you were raised, or what you believe. Whether it is alcohol, street drugs, or pain pills, I have seen these substances take men and women to places they never imagined. I was one of them. I battled addiction for more than twenty-one years, and this is how I learned to take life one day at a time.

In the late 1980s, crack cocaine swept through communities like a wildfire. It was cheap, easy to get, and it destroyed lives faster than anything I had ever seen. In 1989, I was introduced to cocaine at a club. Back then, everyone was doing it. We had crack-smoking parties. At first, it seemed harmless, even fun.

That illusion did not last long.

By January of 1990, I was back to smoking crack, and this time the police entered my life. I was arrested at a car wash in my hometown and thrown into jail. Because my bond was too high for my family to pay, I sat in that cell for seventy-eight days. I slept on a hard bunk with a thin mattress, a torn sheet, and half of a blanket. The only thing I had to hold onto was a small blue New Testament Bible.

I began to read it from the beginning, day after day. That was when I started learning who the Lord was and what He could do. I kept coming back to the story of Paul and Silas in jail, how an angel of the Lord broke their chains and opened the doors. I did not understand it fully then, but something in me knew I was reading about freedom.

One day, after returning from a doctor's appointment, I found the detective who had arrested me standing in front of my cell. He asked how much my bond was and what property my family owned. When I told him, he said, "That's your bond." And just like that, I was released.

At the time, I did not give God the credit. I thought man had the power. I walked out of jail after seventy-eight days still blind in my faith.

It did not take long for the cravings to return. I went back to crack cocaine, and this time I hit bottom even harder. Before long, I was right back in that same jail, sitting on that same hard bunk, ashamed and empty. I had nowhere left to run.

1

A Life Before the Drugs

Before addiction ever took hold of my life, there was already something missing inside me. I grew up knowing there was a God. I was raised around church, Sunday school, and the idea that there was a higher power watching over us. I went to Baptist churches, heard the sermons, sang the songs, and believed in God the way a child believes, simply because that was what I was taught.

But belief and understanding are not the same thing.

As I grew into my teenage years, something in me started to feel restless. I did not know how to name it at the time. I just knew I did not feel settled inside myself. I would look at people who seemed confident and happy, and I could not understand why I felt different. Even though I was surrounded by family and familiar places, I carried a quiet emptiness that followed me everywhere.

In my early twenties, I began drifting. I went from one environment to another, from church to the streets, from hope to confusion. Some days I was trying to live right. Other days I was just trying to escape how I felt. I was curious about different beliefs, different lifestyles, and different ways of thinking. I was searching for something, though I did not know what it was.

I still believed in God, but I did not know Him.

I went to church, but I did not live like it. I could sit in a pew on Sunday and then turn around and make choices that pulled me farther away from peace during the rest of the week. I was learning how to survive, not how to live. And that survival mindset would later open the door to something much darker.

By the late 1980s, the world around me was changing. Crack cocaine was everywhere. It was cheap, easy to get, and spreading fast through my community. People I knew were using it openly. It became part of the culture, part of the scene, part of what it meant to fit in. At first, I watched from a distance. Then one night in 1989, at a club, I joined in.

It did not feel dangerous at first. It felt exciting. It felt like connection. It felt like escape. Back then, we even had what people called crack-smoking parties. Everyone was doing it. No one was talking about addiction, jail, or death. We were just chasing a feeling.

That was how it started.

What I did not know then was that I had just stepped onto a road that would take me through jails, institutions, broken relationships, and years of pain before I ever found my way back. I thought I was in control. I thought I was just having fun.

But addiction was already learning my name.

2

The First High

By the time I walked into that club in 1989, I had no idea my life was about to change forever. Back then, cocaine was everywhere. Crack cocaine had taken over the streets, especially in communities like mine. It was cheap. It was easy to get. And it was destroying people faster than anything I had ever seen, even if most of us did not realize it yet.

At the time, nobody was talking about addiction. Nobody was warning us about what would happen. People were just doing it. We had crack-smoking parties. It was part of the scene. It was part of how people connected. If you wanted to belong, this was what you did.

I tried cocaine that year at a club. I remember thinking it was just something everyone did. It felt exciting. It felt like a release. It made me forget the restlessness inside me, at least for a little while. For the first time in a long time, I felt like I fit in.

That feeling was what I started chasing.

I was able to stop for a while. I stayed off crack for about a year. I told myself I was fine, that I had it under control. But control is one of the first things addiction takes from you without you noticing.

In January of 1990, I went back to smoking crack. That was when everything started to unravel.

Not long after, the police got involved in my life. I was arrested at a car wash in my hometown. When they took me in, I did not think much about it at first. I still believed I could manage my situation. I still believed I was in charge.

I was wrong.

Because my bond was high and my family could not afford to post bail, I stayed in jail for seventy-eight days. Seventy-eight days in a small cell with a hard bunk, a thin mattress, a torn sheet, and half of a blanket. That was all I had. I was cold, tired, and alone.

The only thing that gave me any comfort was a small blue New Testament Bible. I started reading it from the beginning. Day after day, I read. I began to learn about who the Lord was and what He could do. I kept coming back to the story of Paul and Silas in jail, how the angel of the Lord had broken their chains and opened the cell doors. I did not fully understand it, but something inside me was drawn to it.

One day, I was taken out of my cell for a doctor's appointment. When I came back, the detective who had arrested me was standing in front of my cell door. He asked me how much my bond was. Then he asked how much property my family owned. When I told him, he said, "That's your bond."

And just like that, I was free.

I walked out of that jail after seventy-eight days. I did not realize it then, but God had already been working in my life. I was reading about Paul and Silas being released by an angel, but I still believed man had the power. I was blind in my faith.

I went home with money still saved. I thought I would be fine. But not long after, the cravings came back. They always came back.

I went right back to crack cocaine.

This time, I fell even harder.

And before I knew it, I was right back in that same jail, sitting on that same hard bunk, feeling ashamed, hungry, lonely, and exhausted. When they opened my cell door and said my name, I knew exactly how far I had fallen.

I had just begun a cycle that would follow me for years.

3

When Control Was Lost

The second time I went back to jail, something inside me started to break. I was sitting on that same hard bunk, in that same cold cell, realizing that nothing had really changed. I had been given freedom, but I did not know what to do with it. I was still chasing the same feeling. I was still running from myself.

When I was released again, I went right back to drinking and using. Alcohol always led me back to crack cocaine. It did not matter how much I promised myself it would be different. It always started out the same way. It felt fun. It felt like an escape. But it never stayed that way.

I was only twenty years old, and already my life was being shaped by addiction. My grandmother, Enola Carter, was the only person who truly cared for me at the time. She loved me deeply and did everything she could to help me, even when I was hurting myself. Looking back, I can see that she was also enabling me, but at the time, I was too lost to understand that.

I began moving through a cycle that would follow me for years. I would drink. I would use. I would fall apart. Then I would go to detox or a treatment center. I would clean myself up just enough to look normal again. And when I was released, I would do the same things all over again, expecting a different result.

It never came.

Every time I left a twenty-eight-day program, I told myself I was ready. But deep inside, I was already thinking about using again. I was afraid to tell the counselors the truth, because I did not want to stay longer. So I would walk out pretending I was strong, when in reality I was already slipping.

Sometimes I would not even make it home before the craving took over.

The disease of addiction is patient. It waits. It does not rush you. It watches until the moment you feel free, and then it strikes. I learned that you can be absent from alcohol or drugs, but the thought is still there. And when that thought is not dealt with, it becomes a relapse before you ever pick up anything.

I went through detox centers, mental health institutions, jails, and halfway houses. I learned about my addiction. I learned about my mental illness. I was given tools to help me cope. But most of the time, none of it worked, because in my subconscious mind the drug was still calling me.

I did not believe I was worth anything. I had jobs, but I would lose them because of my drinking and my crack cocaine use. My relationships never lasted. I drove people away, including women who tried to care about me and family members who wanted to help. Living in a small town, everyone knew I was addicted. I was becoming known for all the wrong reasons.

When my grandmother died on June 12, 1996, I was completely alone. The one person who had always stood by me was gone. After that, I started getting locked up even more. My life was headed straight toward destruction, and I could feel it happening, but I did not know how to stop.

My daughter was growing up without me. I was missing her life while I destroyed my own. I tried to just drink instead of using drugs, but alcohol always led me right back to crack. No matter how much I learned in treatment, no matter how much I promised myself to change, I kept falling into the same pattern.

I was losing everything that mattered, one relapse at a time.

And I did not yet know that things were still going to get worse before they ever got better.

4

The Jail Cell

There is something about being locked in a jail cell that forces you to face yourself. You cannot run. You cannot hide. All you have is time, silence, and your own thoughts. For me, that cell became a place where everything I had been avoiding finally caught up to me.

I had been arrested again and was sitting in the same jail I had been in before. My charge this time was contempt of court. They gave me thirty days. Thirty days to sit on a hard bunk, in a cold room, with nothing but a thin mattress, a torn sheet, and half of a blanket. I was tired, hungry, and ashamed.

When they opened my cell door for chow, they said my name and laughed, "You back again?" I felt the weight of that question. I was numb. All I wanted to do was eat and escape the nightmare that had become my life. But there was nowhere left to escape to.

After breakfast, I went back to my cell and picked up that same blue New Testament Bible. I began reading it from front to back, just like I had before. I did not know what else to do. I had no money, no freedom, and no answers. But I had that Bible.

Day after day, I read. I learned about who the Lord was and what He could do. I kept coming back to the story of Paul and Silas, how they had been locked up and how an angel of the Lord had come and broken their chains. I saw myself in that story, even though I did not fully understand it yet.

When my thirty days were over, they took me to court. I was nervous, expecting the worst. But nothing bad happened. The matter was resolved, and I was sent home.

Once again, I walked out of jail with my freedom.

And once again, I went right back to the same pattern. I started drinking. That led me back to crack cocaine. It always did. It started out feeling like fun, but it never stayed that way. Before long, I was right back where I had been before, lost and broken.

I was learning something I did not want to accept. Jail was not my problem. Drugs were not my only problem. The real problem was inside me. No matter how many times

I got locked up or sent to treatment, I carried the same mind with me everywhere I went.

And that mind kept leading me back to the same place.

5

Blind to Grace

Looking back now, I can see that God was working in my life long before I ever knew it. Even when I was locked in a cell, reading that little blue New Testament, something was being planted inside me. But at the time, I could not see it.

When I walked out of jail after those thirty days, I thought I had been given another chance because of people, courts, or luck. I did not understand that grace had already been at work. I was still blind to what God was doing in my life.

I had read the story of Paul and Silas over and over, how the angel of the Lord had broken their chains and opened the prison doors. I had seen it happen in my own life, too. I had been released when there was no reason I should have been. But instead of giving God the credit, I believed that man had the power.

That blindness kept me trapped.

Freedom without understanding is dangerous. When you do not know why you were spared, you do not know how to live differently. I walked out of jail with money still saved, with another chance to start over. But the craving for crack cocaine came back, just like it always did.

I told myself I would not go back. I told myself it would be different. But addiction does not listen to promises. It listens to desire.

Before long, I was using again. I fell harder than before. And once again, I found myself sitting in that same jail, facing the same shame, the same hunger, the same loneliness. It felt like I was trapped in a cycle that I could not escape.

Each time I came out, I went right back in. Each time I tried to stand, I fell again. I was free on the outside, but I was still locked up on the inside.

I did not know yet that God was not just opening doors. He was trying to change my heart.

But I was not ready to see it.

6

Relapse

Every time I came out of jail or a treatment center, I told myself it would be different. I would look better. I would feel stronger. I would promise everyone, including myself, that I was done. But deep inside, something was still broken.

I would go to detox to get my appearance back. I would stay in a twenty-eight-day program, go through the motions, learn the rules, and listen to the counselors. I knew what I was supposed to say. I knew what I was supposed to do. But the truth was, I was not being honest with myself.

As my release date got closer, the cravings would come. I would start thinking about alcohol. I would start thinking about crack cocaine. I was afraid to tell anyone, because I did not want to stay longer. So I kept quiet. I walked out pretending I was ready, even though I was already losing the fight in my mind.

That is how relapse begins.

Sometimes I would not even make it back to a safe place before I used again. Other times it would take a few days. But the pattern was always the same. Freedom would come, and then the disease of addiction would patiently wait for the moment I let my guard down.

You can be absent from drugs or alcohol, but the thought is always there. And when that thought is not dealt with, it becomes a decision. Before long, I would be right back where I started, drinking and smoking crack, wondering how I had fallen so fast.

I kept expecting different results while doing the same things. I went from detox to treatment to jail and back again. Every time I got a little clean, I thought I had won. But the disease was only waiting for another chance.

Addiction is smart. It knows when you are tired. It knows when you feel free. It knows when you stop paying attention. That is when it moves.

I wanted to change. I really did. I tried long-term treatment centers. I went to programs for my addiction and my mental illness. I learned about triggers and cravings. I learned about tools and coping skills. But most of the time, when I walked out the door, all of that knowledge disappeared.

I was still living with the same thinking that got me there.

And that thinking kept pulling me back into the same darkness, over and over again.

7

Detox, Institutions, and Despair

By this point in my life, I was no longer surprised when I ended up back in a hospital, a detox center, or a jail. It had become normal. I moved through these places like a revolving door, going in and out, never really free.

Every institution taught me something about my addiction and my mental illness. I learned what cravings were. I learned what triggers were. I learned about coping skills. I learned what I was supposed to do to stay sober. But knowing and doing are two different things.

Most of the time, I did not use the tools I was given. As soon as I hit the door to freedom, everything I had learned seemed to disappear. I would walk out thinking I was strong, but inside I was already tired. And when I got tired, the disease of addiction took over.

Sometimes I would relapse in my mind before I ever picked up a drink or a drug. I would start thinking about using. I would start telling myself it would be okay. By the time I actually used, the decision had already been made.

I went through mental health institutions, detox programs, and long-term treatment centers. I was educated about my condition. I was told what to do. But I still kept going back to the same places, the same people, and the same habits. I was living in insanity, doing the same thing over and over and expecting different results.

I did not feel like I had any real value. I thought I was worthless. I would get jobs, but I could not keep them because of my drinking and my crack cocaine use. I destroyed everything I touched. Relationships never lasted. People who tried to help me eventually walked away.

I was becoming more alone with every relapse.

Even when I tried to do better, I still found myself back in the same darkness. I could go weeks or even months without using, but the thought never left. And sooner or later, that thought always won.

I was tired. I was empty. And I was losing hope.

I did not know it yet, but I was being pushed toward a breaking point. A place where I would either change or be destroyed.

8

The Disease That Waits

Addiction is not loud all the time. Most people think it is, but it is not. It is patient. It waits. It does not have to chase you. It only has to be there when you let your guard down.

I learned that the hard way.

There were times when I was clean. I would be out of detox. I would be out of treatment. I would even be doing better for a while. But in my mind, the thought was always there. It would whisper that one drink would not hurt. That one hit would not matter. That I deserved a break.

Those thoughts were more dangerous than the drugs themselves.

I could go to meetings. I could sit in group sessions. I could nod my head and say all the right things. But as soon as I stepped outside, I was back in the same places, around the same people, with the same temptations. And sooner or later, the disease would get its chance.

Most of us in recovery know what we are supposed to do. We know about sponsors. We know about calling for help. We know about staying away from people and places that pull us down. But when the craving hits, all of that knowledge disappears. The disease tells you that you are different. That you can handle it. That this time will not be the same.

It always lies.

I saw people leave treatment and never come back. I saw others relapse again and again until they disappeared completely. Some ended up in prison. Some ended up dead. Some just faded away.

I was still alive, but I was not really living.

I kept trying to fight the disease with willpower, and willpower was never enough. I could not think my way out of addiction. I could not promise my way out of it. No matter how much I wanted to change, something inside me kept pulling me back.

I was learning that addiction was not just about what I did. It was about how I thought.

And until my thinking changed, nothing else would.

9

Losing Everything

By the time I understood how far my addiction had taken me, most of what mattered in my life was already gone. I was not just losing days or jobs. I was losing people. I was losing relationships. I was losing myself.

My daughter was growing up without me. I was not there the way a father should be. I missed moments I would never get back, because I was too busy trying to survive my own chaos. Every time I looked at my life, I felt more ashamed, but shame never made me stop. It only made me hide.

Women would come into my life, hoping I would be different. They saw something in me I could not see in myself. But my drug use drove them away. Addiction made me unreliable, unpredictable, and emotionally distant. No matter how much someone cared, I always chose the drugs and alcohol over them.

My family was hurt, too. They watched me destroy myself, and there was nothing they could do to stop it. In a small town, everyone knew what I was struggling with. I became known for all the wrong reasons. My reputation followed me wherever I went.

I would get jobs and lose them. I would try to rebuild and then tear everything down again. I was living without pride, without direction, and without hope. The more I failed, the more worthless I felt. And the more worthless I felt, the more I used.

It was a cycle that fed itself.

When my grandmother Enola Carter died, the last stable thing in my life disappeared. She had always been there for me, even when I was hurting myself. When she was gone, I felt completely alone. That loneliness pushed me deeper into my addiction.

I was headed toward destruction. I could feel it. My life was becoming smaller and darker. I was losing everything that made me human.

And still, I kept using.

10

My Grandmother

There was one person who never gave up on me, no matter how far I fell. That was my grandmother, Enola Carter.

She loved me in a way that went beyond words. Even when I was lost in my addiction, she still believed there was something good in me. She took care of me when no one else would. She made sure I had a place to stay, food to eat, and someone who still cared whether I lived or died.

Looking back now, I can see that her love was mixed with enabling. She protected me from the full consequences of my actions. She made it easier for me to keep going the way I was. But at the time, all I knew was that she was there for me when the rest of the world was not.

She was the last steady thing in my life.

When she died on June 12, 1996, something inside me broke. I was not just losing a grandmother. I was losing my anchor. I felt like I had been cut loose in the world with nothing to hold onto. After she was gone, I started getting locked up more often. I stopped caring what happened to me.

Her death left a hole in my life that I did not know how to fill. And instead of facing that pain, I ran deeper into drugs and alcohol. I did not know how to grieve. I only knew how to escape.

I wish now that she could see the man I have become. I wish she could know that her love was not wasted. But at the time, all I could feel was the emptiness she left behind.

Her passing marked the end of one part of my life.

And the beginning of the darkest part.

11

The Breaking Point

After my grandmother died, there was nothing left in my life to keep me steady. I was drifting from one disaster to the next, pushing myself deeper into addiction and despair. I was getting locked up more often. I was losing whatever little stability I still had. I did not care anymore what happened to me.

I was tired of being tired. I was tired of running. I was tired of failing. But I did not know how to stop.

My mental health was getting worse along with my addiction. I was moving through jails, detoxes, and institutions like it was normal. Sometimes I would find a little hope, but it never lasted. The moment I felt free, the disease would pull me back.

I knew I was headed for destruction. I could feel it. I was causing damage to myself and everyone around me. I was losing my family, my relationships, and my future. My daughter was growing up without me, and that pain stayed with me even when I was high.

I had reached a point where I could no longer pretend things were going to get better on their own. My life was not just broken. It was falling apart.

I was at war with myself, and I was losing.

There came a moment when I finally saw the truth. I could not keep living like this. I could not keep surviving one crisis just to fall into the next. I was either going to change, or I was going to die.

That was the breaking point.

12

Surrender

I used to think surrender meant giving up. I thought it meant weakness. But when I finally reached the end of myself, I realized it meant something else. It meant letting go of the fight I was losing.

I had tried everything I knew how to try. I had been to detox. I had been to treatment centers. I had been locked up and released more times than I could count. I had promised myself, my family, and God that I would change. And every time, I fell again.

That was when I finally admitted the truth. I could not do this by myself.

I surrendered to the Lord because I had no other place left to go. I stopped trying to control everything. I stopped pretending I had all the answers. I asked God to take over, especially in my mind, where most of the battle had always been.

For the first time, I was honest. I was honest about my addiction. I was honest about my fear. I was honest about my weakness. And in that honesty, something began to shift.

I gave myself to a simple program of recovery. I went to Alcoholics Anonymous. I committed to ninety meetings in ninety days. I found a sponsor. I started working the twelve steps. I did not just listen anymore. I started doing.

I also began taking care of my mental health. I stayed on my medication. I went to therapy. I stopped pretending I did not need help. I learned that healing was not just spiritual. It was emotional and mental too.

Surrender did not make my life perfect. But it gave me a new foundation. Instead of fighting everything, I started trusting something greater than myself.

That was the moment I began to change.

13

AA, NA, and the Steps

After I surrendered, I realized something important. Wanting to change was not enough. I had to live differently. That was where Alcoholics Anonymous and Narcotics Anonymous came into my life in a real way.

I committed to going to meetings. I did ninety meetings in ninety days. I listened to people who had been where I was and had made it out. I heard stories that sounded just like mine. For the first time, I did not feel so alone.

I got a sponsor. I learned that recovery was not meant to be done by myself. When I was struggling, I had someone I could call. When I was confused, I had someone who could guide me. I began working the twelve steps, one day at a time.

The steps taught me how to be honest with myself. They taught me how to look at my past without running from it. They taught me how to take responsibility for the harm I had done and how to begin making things right.

One of the hardest lessons was learning to change the people I spent time with. I was told to choose my friends carefully and to stay away from places that pulled me back into my old life. I was also warned not to get into a relationship for at least a year, because most addicts relapse when they stop focusing on their recovery.

That was true.

When people start to feel better, they often stop doing what kept them well. They stop going to meetings. They stop calling their sponsor. They start putting someone else ahead of their recovery. And before long, they end up right back where they started.

I learned that I had to protect my sobriety. It had to come first. Not my pride. Not my desires. Not my relationships.

Recovery became something I practiced every day. And little by little, I stayed clean.

14

Mental Health

Getting sober did not fix everything in my life. It was the beginning, not the end. Along with addiction, I had been carrying mental illness for many years. If I wanted to stay clean, I had to take care of my mind as well as my spirit.

I learned that there was no shame in needing help. I went to therapy. I stayed on my medication. I became what doctors call "med compliant." That meant I took what I was prescribed and did not try to do things my own way. For the first time, my mind began to settle.

Before that, my thoughts had always been scattered. Fear, anger, confusion, and pride controlled me. But with treatment and prayer, things started to change. I could think more clearly. I could slow down. I could face situations without feeling like I was going to fall apart.

Some people believe faith alone should fix everything. I believe faith and responsibility go together. God gave doctors wisdom for a reason. When I did my part and took care of my mental health, I was able to stay balanced and strong in my recovery.

I stopped living on the edge of chaos. I stopped waking up afraid of what the day would bring. My life became more stable. I could keep appointments. I could show up for people. I could be present.

Taking care of my mental health was not weakness. It was survival. And it allowed me to keep moving forward in my sobriety and in my faith.

15

A New Mind

Something slowly began to change inside me as I stayed sober and took care of my mental health. My thoughts were not as dark as they used to be. I was no longer trapped in the same patterns that had kept me sick for so long. It felt like my mind was being renewed.

I started to see life differently. I stopped living in constant fear of going back to where I came from. I stopped worrying about my past all the time. The more I focused on doing the right thing each day, the more peaceful I became.

I learned that I was my own worst enemy. I had been the one putting myself in jail, treatment centers, and dangerous situations. When I accepted that truth, I also realized I could make different choices.

I set goals for myself. Some were small. Some were bigger. But for the first time, I was actually reaching them. My main goal was simple: stay sober. Everything else came after that.

I also learned how to forgive. I forgave myself for the damage I had done. I forgave the people who had hurt me. I let go of resentment, because I finally understood how heavy it was to carry.

As my mind changed, my life changed. I did not go to the same places anymore. I did not spend time with the same people. My circle became smaller, but it became safer.

I was learning how to live again.

16

Fourteen Years Sober

On May 4, 2011, my life changed in a way I never thought was possible. That was the day I became sober, and today I have fourteen years without alcohol or drugs. I do not say that with pride. I say it with gratitude.

Staying sober is not about being strong. It is about being honest. I do not put myself in fragile situations anymore. I do not go to places that pull me back toward my old life. I still talk to my sponsor. I still go to therapy. I still take my medication. I still pray.

My life today is not complicated. I take things one day at a time.

The desire to use cocaine or drink alcohol is gone. That does not mean temptation never comes. It means I have learned how to respond when it does. I do not let negativity control me. I do not hold on to resentment. I forgive quickly.

I am a pastor now, well known in Louisiana. I serve the Lord and do my best to live by what I preach. I have peace in my life that I never had before.

My relationships have been restored. My daughter is back in my life. Her mother and I are friends. My family supports me. I am no longer pushing people away.

I still have ups and downs. I am still human. But the ups far outweigh the downs now.

Fourteen years ago, I was broken.
Today, I am free.

17

Ministry

When God changed my life, He did not just free me from addiction. He gave me a calling. I became a pastor and began preaching the truth of what God had done for me. I did not preach from theory. I preached from experience. I knew what it meant to be broken, and I knew what it meant to be delivered.

I started a worship service online. I spoke to people who were struggling, people who felt lost, people who were still caught in addiction and despair. I told them what I had lived. I told them that if God could change me, He could change anyone.

My ministry has an anointing on it. I see God drawing people to me. I do not chase them. I do not force anything. I let God do the work. My job is to stay faithful.

I still pray every day. I still fast. I still study the Bible. I still listen for the voice of the Holy Spirit. That quiet, still voice guides me and keeps me from going back to who I used to be.

There was a time when people thought I would be dead, locked up, or out of my mind. Now those same people look at me and cannot believe the change. That is not my doing. That is God.

My ministry is not about money or fame. It is about saving lives. It is about showing people that freedom is real.

And I live that truth every day.

18

Family Restored

One of the greatest gifts God gave me when I got sober was my family back. For many years, addiction had separated me from the people who mattered most. I had hurt them. I had disappointed them. I had been absent when I should have been present. But when I began to change, they saw it. And little by little, relationships were restored.

My daughter is back in my life. We talk, we text, and we support each other. I tell her every chance I get how much I love her and how proud I am of her. Her mother and I are friends now, something I never thought would be possible. There is peace where there used to be pain.

My nieces and nephews believe in me. They are proud of me. I am proud of them. We share love, laughter, and memories that addiction once stole from me.

My brothers and sisters support me. We talk. We stay connected. We have real relationships now, not the broken ones I used to have.

There was a time when I thought I had lost my family forever. But God restored what addiction tried to destroy.

That restoration is one of the greatest miracles of my life.

19

What God Taught Me

God did not just save me from addiction. He taught me how to live. He taught me that pride and control were some of my greatest enemies. I always wanted things my way. I wanted to be in charge. But when I let go and let God lead, my life finally found peace.

I learned that forgiveness is freedom. When I forgave myself for the harm I had done, and when I forgave others who had hurt me, something inside me was released. I was no longer chained to the past.

God taught me to be patient. He taught me to wait. He taught me that not everything has to be rushed. When I trust Him, things fall into place.

I learned that faith is not just something you talk about. It is something you live. It is in the choices you make when no one is watching. It is in the way you treat people. It is in the way you respond to pain.

God also taught me that my story has a purpose. The pain I went through was not wasted. It became a testimony that can help someone else.

Everything I went through led me here.

And I am grateful.

20

For the One Still Using

If you are reading this and you are still using, I want you to know something. I have been where you are. I know what it feels like to wake up sick, ashamed, and afraid. I know what it feels like to want to stop but not know how.

You are not weak. You are not broken beyond repair. You are not alone.

Addiction lies to you. It tells you that you are different. It tells you that you cannot change. It tells you that no one cares. But that is not true. I was told the same lies, and I believed them for years.

You do not have to do this by yourself. Reach out. Go to a meeting. Call someone. Pray. Be honest. The moment you ask for help, something begins to shift.

God does not see you the way you see yourself. He sees who you can become. I was lost, addicted, and mentally ill, and God still changed me. If He could do it for me, He can do it for you.

Do not wait until everything is gone. Do not wait until the pain is unbearable. There is another way to live.

Take it one day at a time.

You are worth saving.

Epilogue:

One Day at a Time

My journey did not end when I got sober. It began. There was a time when I lived just to survive. Every day was about getting through the pain, the cravings, and the chaos inside my mind. I never thought I would know peace. I never thought I would feel whole.

But today, I wake up with something to live for.

I still take my medication. I still go to therapy. I still pray. I still talk to my sponsor. I still take life one day at a time. Those things keep me grounded and honest. They remind me that I do not have to be perfect to be free.

I no longer live in my past. I do not let yesterday control today. I have learned that when you focus on the moment you are in, life becomes simpler. The fear fades. The noise quiets. And you can finally breathe.

God restored what addiction tried to destroy. He gave me my family back. He gave me purpose. He gave me peace. Most of all, He gave me myself.

There are still challenges. There are still hard days. But I am no longer alone in them. I face them with faith, with support, and with the knowledge that I do not have to go back to who I used to be.

If this book has taught me anything, it is this.

No matter how far you have fallen, you can rise. No matter how broken you feel, you can be made whole. No matter how dark it gets, there is still light.

Take it one day at a time.

Your journey can begin again, too.

Made in the USA
Coppell, TX
13 February 2026

72016714R00035